Little People, **BIG DREAMS**™

WILMA MANKILLER

Written by
Maria Isabel Sánchez Vegara

Illustrated by
Alexandra Bowman

Frances Lincoln
Children's Books

Once in Oklahoma there was a thoughtful girl called Wilma. She was a proud member of the Cherokee tribe. Her people had lived in America for thousands of years before European settlers arrived and took their land.

Under threats and false promises, her ancestors were forced to
leave their homes and walk to land set aside for them. It was
named "Indian Territory" by the government. The trip was so hard
that those lucky enough to make it called it "The Trail of Tears."

Things had got better, but life was still tough for Wilma's family. They were so poor that her mother used flour sacks to make clothes, and the eleven siblings had to hunt, fish, and pick peanuts to bring food to the table every day.

Her family—like many others—was persuaded by the government to leave their land and move to San Francisco, the big city. Suddenly, Wilma was leaving not just her friends behind but her roots, too. It was her own little Trail of Tears.

Wilma and her siblings were the only Native Americans at her new school. Sadly, most students bullied them and made fun of their last name. So she ran away and completed high school after living with her grandmother for a year.

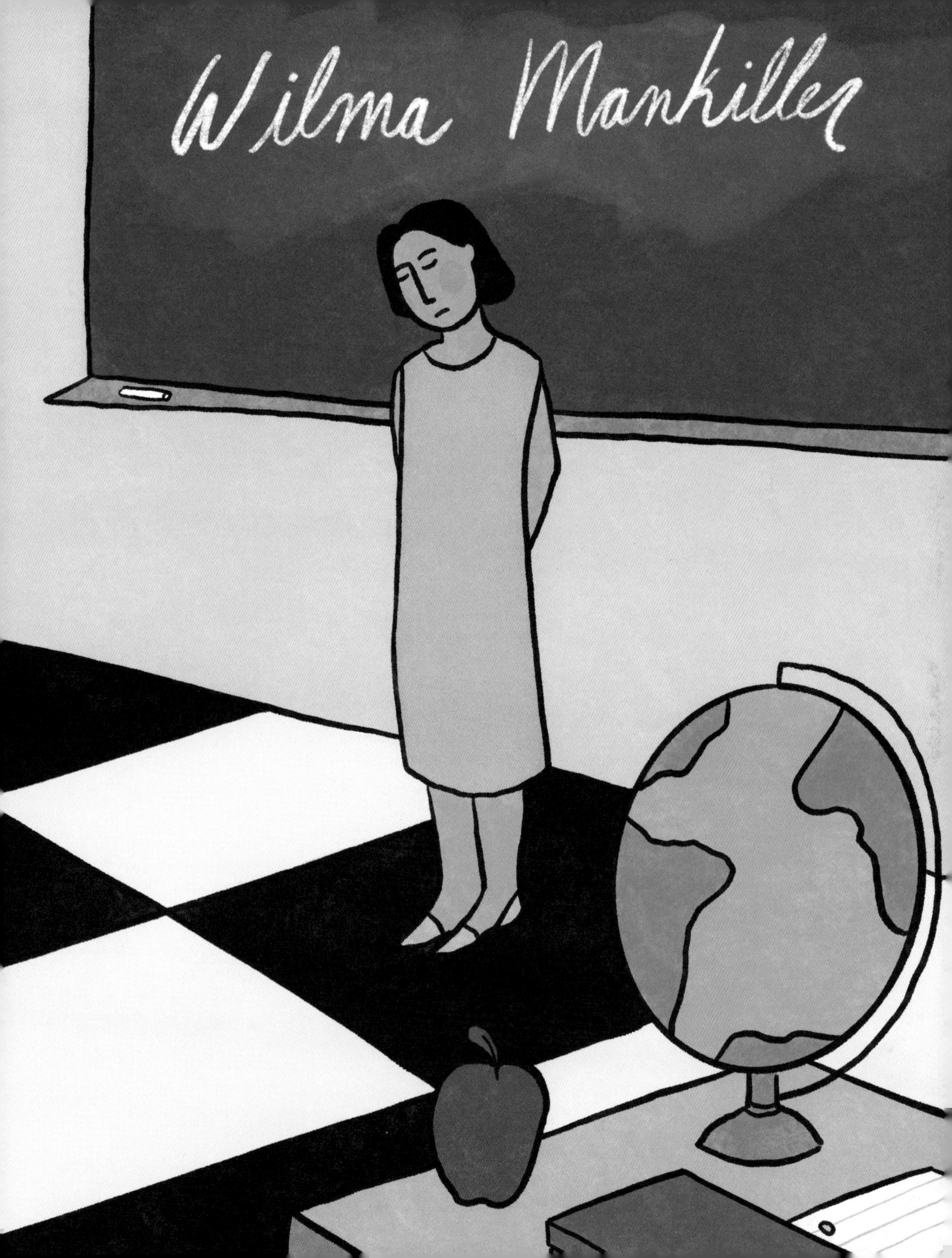
Wilma Mankiller

One day, at a Latin dance, she met a guy named Hugo. Once they married, her husband expected her to stay at home to take care of their two daughters. Still, Wilma dreamt of making a difference in her community, too.

Her life changed when Native American demonstrators took over Alcatraz, an island in San Francisco Bay. They called attention to the government's mistreatment of their people, and Wilma joined them in raising money for the cause.

She began taking night courses in college and used all she had learned to organise activities and programs for the Indigenous students in her community.

But her husband was not happy with her choice,
and they finally split up.

Back in Oklahoma, she fell in love again and got a job with the Cherokee Nation, one of the largest tribes in the United States. Wilma worked so hard to improve the lives of her people that the tribe's Principal Chief asked her to be his right hand.

Two years later, Wilma succeeded him as the tribe's leader, becoming the first female Principal Chief. She led the Cherokee Nation for ten years, fighting to protect the environment and working toward an equal relationship with the US government.

Some members of the tribe didn't like having a woman in charge, but the eldest of them became Wilma's biggest supporters. They knew that Cherokee women and men had shared the power before. It was time to get the harmony back!

Even after she left office, the tribal leaders kept seeking her advice. She always told them to follow the "Cherokee approach" to life, by focusing on the good things and thinking that every day is a great day if you want it to be.

And every summer as they celebrate their roots, the whole Cherokee Nation remembers little Wilma: the girl who knew that the happiest people are those who care about others, and who stand for something larger than themselves.

WILMA MANKILLER

(Born 1945 – Died 2010)

1986

1992

Wilma Pearl Mankiller, a member of the Cherokee Nation, was born in Tahlequah, Oklahoma. She grew up on a farm assigned to her grandfather after the US government forced him and others to leave tribal land, on an arduous, deadly journey known as "The Trail of Tears." The farm had no electricity or plumbing, and the Mankillers foraged for food and made their own clothes. A government program, designed to break up Native American communities, encouraged them and other families to move away from their land to San Francisco. They were made lots of promises about housing and jobs that didn't come true. In the 1960s, she was inspired by Native American activists who were fighting for their civil rights, such as the right to live on ancestral land. Wilma became

1998

2005

involved with activism herself and raised money for people protesting at Alcatraz, a small island off the coast of San Francisco. After her marriage ended, Wilma returned to Oklahoma with her two daughters and began working for the Cherokee Nation. Despite facing discrimination for being female, she was elected as Deputy Chief and then Principal Chief of the tribe, becoming the first woman to ever take the role. During her ten years in leadership, she worked to improve standards of education and health care for her people. When her time in office came to an end, Wilma served the community in a different way by teaching Native American studies. A believer in positive thinking and decisive action, Wilma is a role model for girls and women everywhere.

Want to find out more about **Wilma Mankiller?**

Have a read of this great book:

Wilma's Way Home: The Life of Wilma Mankiller
by Doreen Rappaport

Brimming with creative inspiration, how-to projects, and useful information to enrich your everyday life, quarto.com is a favourite destination for those pursuing their interests and passions.

Published by Peter Marley • Designed by Sasha Moxon

Edited by Lucy Menzies • Production by Nikki Ingram

Editorial Assistance from Rachel Robinson

Manufactured in Guangdong, China CC042022

1 3 5 7 9 8 6 4 2

Photographic acknowledgements (pages 28-29, from left to right): 1. Photograph used for a story in the Daily Oklahoman newspaper. Caption: "Cherokee Nation Principal Chief Wilma P. Mankiller, inducted into Oklahoma Women's Hall of Fame" October 12, 1986 © Oklahoma Historical Society. 2. Wilma Mankiller, principal chief of the Cherokee Nation, poses beside a lake. Mankiller was the first female principal chief in the history of the Cherokee Nation. © Peter Turnley/Corbis via Getty Images. 3. US President Bill Clinton (R) places the Presidential Medal of Freedom, the nation's highest civilian honor, around the neck of Wilma Mankiller (L) 15 January during ceremonies at the White House in Washington, DC. Mankiller, who was twice elected to head the Cherokee Nation in the US, received the honor for her work to reduce infant mortality, improve health and education and promote business among Cherokees. © Paul J Richards/AFP via Getty Images. 4. Writer Wilma Mankiller, who was honored at the event, attends the American Indian College Fund Gala at the Museum of the American West on May 20, 2005 in Los Angeles, California. © Stephen Shugerman/Stringer via Getty Images

Collect the *Little People,* **BIG DREAMS™** series:

FRIDA KAHLO	**COCO CHANEL**	**MAYA ANGELOU**	**AMELIA EARHART**	**AGATHA CHRISTIE**	**MARIE CURIE**	**ROSA PARKS**	**AUDREY HEPBURN**

EMMELINE PANKHURST	**ELLA FITZGERALD**	**ADA LOVELACE**	**JANE AUSTEN**	**GEORGIA O'KEEFFE**	**HARRIET TUBMAN**	**ANNE FRANK**	**MOTHER TERESA**

JOSEPHINE BAKER	**L. M. MONTGOMERY**	**JANE GOODALL**	**SIMONE DE BEAUVOIR**	**MUHAMMAD ALI**	**STEPHEN HAWKING**	**MARIA MONTESSORI**	**VIVIENNE WESTWOOD**

MAHATMA GANDHI	**DAVID BOWIE**	**WILMA RUDOLPH**	**DOLLY PARTON**	**BRUCE LEE**	**RUDOLF NUREYEV**	**ZAHA HADID**	**MARY SHELLEY**

MARTIN LUTHER KING JR.	**DAVID ATTENBOROUGH**	**ASTRID LINDGREN**	**EVONNE GOOLAGONG**	**BOB DYLAN**	**ALAN TURING**	**BILLIE JEAN KING**	**GRETA THUNBERG**

JESSE OWENS	**JEAN-MICHEL BASQUIAT**	**ARETHA FRANKLIN**	**CORAZON AQUINO**	**PELÉ**	**ERNEST SHACKLETON**	**STEVE JOBS**	**AYRTON SENNA**

LOUISE BOURGEOIS	**ELTON JOHN**	**JOHN LENNON**	**PRINCE**	**CHARLES DARWIN**	**CAPTAIN TOM MOORE**	**HANS CHRISTIAN ANDERSEN**	**STEVIE WONDER**

MEGAN RAPINOE	MARY ANNING	MALALA YOUSAFZAI	ANDY WARHOL	RUPAUL	MICHELLE OBAMA	MINDY KALING	IRIS APFEL

ROSALIND FRANKLIN	RUTH BADER GINSBURG	MARILYN MONROE	KAMALA HARRIS	ALBERT EINSTEIN	CHARLES DICKENS	YOKO ONO	MICHAEL JORDAN

NELSON MANDELA	PABLO PICASSO	AMANDA GORMAN	GLORIA STEINEM	FLORENCE NIGHTINGALE	HARRY HOUDINI	J.R.R. TOLKIEN	ELVIS PRESLEY

NEIL ARMSTRONG	ALEXANDER VON HUMBOLDT	NIKOLA TESLA	WILMA MANKILLER	MARCUS RASHFORD	LAVERNE COX	MAE JEMISON

ACTIVITY BOOKS

STICKER ACTIVITY BOOK   COLORING BOOK   LITTLE ME, BIG DREAMS JOURNAL

Discover more about the series at www.littlepeoplebigdreams.com